QA 0749 **655402** 9001 ✓

Dun Laoghaire-Rathdown Libraries
SHANKILL LIBRARY
Inv/04 : I290J   Price €19.19
Title: Israel and Palestine
Class:

J956.94

D0190602

ISRAEL AND PALESTINE

MICHAEL GALLAGHER

W

FRANKLIN WATTS
LONDON•SYDNEY

Designer Steve Prosser
Editor Louisa Sladen
Art Director Jonathan Hair
Editor-in-Chief John C. Miles
Picture Research Diana Morris
Map artwork Ian Thompson

© 2004 Franklin Watts

First published in 2004
by Franklin Watts
96 Leonard Street
London
EC2A 4XD

Franklin Watts Australia
45-51 Huntley Street
Alexandria
NSW 2015

ISBN 0 7496 5540 2

A CIP catalogue record for this book is
available from the British Library.

Printed in Malaysia

Picture credits
Bettmann/Corbis: 11t, 14b, 22b, 23t
Sigurd Bojesen/Popperfoto: 30b
Stephanie Colasanti/Corbis: 8b
Darryl Heikes/Popperfoto: 33t
Gary Hershorn/Popperfoto: back cover, 38b
Jim Hollander/Reuters/Popperfoto: 36b
Gil Cohen Magen/Reuters/Popperfoto: 40c
Buddy Mays/Corbis: front cover t, 9t
Francoise de Mulder/Corbis: front cover b, 28c
Popperfoto: 12c, 13c, 15t, 17c, 18b, 19t, 20c, 21t,
25t, 27t, 29t, 31b
Reuters/Popperfoto: 16b
Sipa Press/Rex Features: 34b
Jon Spaull/Panos Pictures: 37t
Walter Wisniewski/Popperfoto: 35t

*Every attempt has been made to clear
copyright. Should there be any inadvertent
omission, please apply to the publisher for
rectification.*

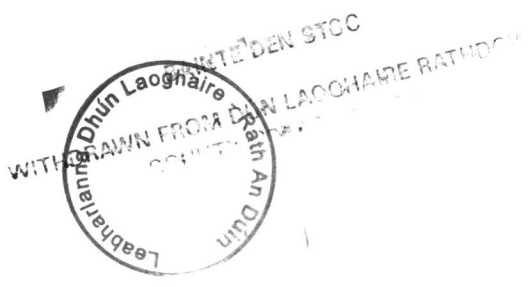

CONTENTS

Israeli Jews and Palestinian Arabs sometimes appear to have so many differences that it can be easy to forget their shared history and suffering. Yet their ancestry – and the roots of their conflict – go back to Biblical times.

CHILDREN OF ABRAHAM

Both Jews and Muslim Arabs believe they are descended from the Old Testament patriarch, Abraham (Ibrahim), who may have lived up to 4,000 years ago. According to Jewish tradition, the twelve tribes of ancient Israel were founded through the descent of Abraham's younger son, Isaac; Muslims believe that his older son, Ishmael, was father of the Arab nation.

THE ISRAELITES

The Israelite tribes first settled in ancient Palestine - then known as Canaan - around 1250 BC, believing that this land had been promised to them by God. Under their kings, David and Solomon, they made the city of Jerusalem their spiritual capital, complete with a splendid temple. The Israelites are said to have become a rich nation, whose borders extended far beyond present-day Israel.

After Solomon's death in the 10th century BC, the Israelites split into two kingdoms: Israel and Judah. To the north, the Kingdom of Israel was overrun by nearby Assyria. Judah, to the south, gave its name to the Jewish people. However, in the 6th century BC, Judah was conquered by the Babylonians. Its most notable citizens were carried off and Jerusalem destroyed. Some seventy years later, the Jews were allowed to return to their land, so fulfilling an ancient prophecy.

PERSECUTION AND EXILE

Over the centuries, Judah came under the control of other conquerors, finally becoming a province of the Roman Empire. Then, after a revolt in AD 66, Jerusalem was again razed to the ground. The Romans banned Jews from the city, and renamed their land *Syria Palaestina*, or Palestine. Shortly afterwards, Christianity emerged as an alternative faith in this, the land of Jesus's life and death. By then, persecution had led many Jews to leave Palestine. The worldwide dispersal of Jews to many different lands - known as the Diaspora - had begun.

The ruins of this ancient synagogue at Capernaum, Israel, date back to Biblical times.

THE ARRIVAL OF ISLAM

In the early 7th century AD a new religion was born in the Arabian peninsula: Islam.

THE IMPORTANCE OF JERUSALEM

The Dome of the Rock mosque, in Jerusalem, is one of Islam's holiest sites.

Jerusalem stands at the centre of today's Arab-Israeli conflict because of its spiritual importance and disputed ownership. Jews trace their stewardship of the city back 3,000 years to when it was the centre of the Israelite kingdom, and say it remains rightfully theirs. However, Christians also revere it as the place where Jesus died, while Muslims say it is holy to them as the site of a miraculous Night Journey to Heaven by the Prophet, Mohammed.

The city boasts some of the most important spiritual places in all three religions, including the Western Wall, the Dome of the Rock mosque (left) and the Church of the Holy Sepulchre. The issue of who should rule Jerusalem is one of the thorniest problems now facing the mainly Jewish Israelis and the mainly Muslim Palestinians.

Islam was brought to Palestine by Arab armies, many of whom remained there and mixed with the existing population. The Muslim Arabs captured Jerusalem, which they, along with Christians and Jews, considered a holy city.

BROTHERS IN SUFFERING

For centuries, Muslim Arabs and Jews lived together in relative harmony, before both fell victim to the European Christians. In 1095, Pope Urban II called for a holy war to reclaim Jerusalem for Christianity, and the First Crusade reached the city four years later. The crusaders unleashed a bloodbath upon Muslims and Jews alike. Nearly ninety years passed before Muslim armies recaptured Jerusalem, but the Christian crusaders' attacks continued for centuries afterwards.

From these early events in Jewish and Arab history, we can see that both peoples were capable of peaceful co-existence. Yet, in the dispersal of the Jews from Palestine and in competition for the holy city of Jerusalem, the seeds of today's conflict were sown.

ANCIENT BACKGROUND

1250 BC Israelite tribes conquer lands of Canaan

993-961 BC Reign of King David; expansion of Israelite land, with Jerusalem as the capital

961-922 BC Reign of King Solomon

722 BC Assyrians destroy northern kingdom of Israel

586 BC Conquest of Judah by Babylonians

333 BC Conquest by Alexander the Great; many Jews leave Palestine

63 BC The Jewish state of Judea (the successor to Judah) becomes part of the Roman Empire

AD 66–73 Revolt of the Jews against Rome, crushed by the Roman emperor, Vespasian

AD 313 The Roman emperor, Constantine, allows Christianity throughout the Empire

ZIONISM

Although ancient Israel had disappeared into history, there were always Jews who kept its memory alive. In modern times, their cause was championed by the 19th-century Zionist movement, which sought to recreate a Jewish state in Palestine.

REMEMBERING GOD'S PROMISE

Arabs became the majority of the population in Palestine, but many Jews still regarded it as their own, God-given land. For some, this was more than just symbolism. Recalling the prophecy that they would return to their homeland after their exile by the Babylonians, some Jews left the Diaspora to settle in the lands of ancient Israel. But even as our modern era dawned, the number of Jews in the region was small.

THE JEWS' DILEMMA

The Jews had by now dispersed throughout much of the world, and their strong sense of identity had often enabled them to forge successful communities in others' lands. Excluded from certain professions, they had become prominent in areas like commerce and the arts. Yet their experience remained one of continued persecution, and even expulsion from the many lands in which they had settled.

Some Jews responded by adopting the cultures they lived within - an idea known as assimilation. They hoped this would make them a less visible target for anti-Semitism. But the old feelings of hostility towards them persisted, especially in eastern Europe. Here, Jews were often confined to certain areas of towns and cities. Then, in the late 19th century, a series of violent anti-Semitic attacks led many Jews all over Europe to believe that assimilation could never work.

A CALL TO RETURN

A feeling grew among some Jews that they needed a home of their own once again. By the end of the 19th century, the Zionist movement was born - a campaign of mass return to the lands around Jerusalem, or Zion. Several other locations were suggested for a homeland, including Uganda and South America; however, Palestine remained the favourite because of its links with Jewish history. Zionism's greatest authority was a Hungarian-born writer called Theodore Herzl. He gathered prominent Jews to discuss the project, and helped establish the World Zionist Organisation, which raised money for Jews to settle in Palestine.

THEODORE HERZL (1860–1904), FATHER OF ZIONISM

Theodore Herzl was born in Hungary, but studied and worked in Vienna. Like many Jews of his time, he initially favoured assimilation with Christian Europe. He changed his mind following a storm of violent anti-Semitism unleashed by the Dreyfus Affair in France, when a Jewish army officer was wrongly charged with treason.

Herzl wrote a book, *Der Judenstaat* (*The Jewish State*), arguing that the Jews' only protection lay in a state of their own, and convened the first Zionist Congress in Basel in 1897 to discuss the idea.

This photograph shows delegates to the World Zionist Congress of 1902 held in Basel, Switzerland. Theodore Herzl is circled, centre.

A few Orthodox Jews opposed the idea of a homeland. They believed that Israel was a state of mind rather than a physical place, and they cited the periodic disasters that befell the ancient Israelites as proof that God agreed. Nevertheless, Zionism grew in strength, appealing to different Jews for different reasons: some wanted a Jewish homeland for religious reasons; some, in order to replace religion with secular nationalism. Others wanted to build a classless utopia. Whatever the impetus, one huge obstacle stood before the 19th-century Zionists: Palestine was not an empty land, as many of them preferred to believe. It had by now been home to the Palestinian Arabs for 1,300 years.

> **'A land without a people for a people without a land.'**
>
> **Zionist slogan**

THE ROAD TO ZION

1881 Massacres of Jews in Russia and Romania lead to the first large-scale Jewish migration, or *aliya*, to Palestine a year later; Jews comprise four per cent of the population

1882 Eliezer Ben-Yehuda creates the modern Hebrew language

1896 Theodore Herzl publishes *Der Judenstaat*

1897 The first Zionist Congress establishes the World Zionist Organisation

1903 Start of second aliya of socialist-Zionists

1905 Following a failed revolution in Russia, anti-Jewish riots take place in hundreds of towns across the country, killing thousands of Jews

1909 Zionists establish Tel Aviv as a Jewish suburb of the Arab city of Jaffa

1918-20 Pogroms take place in Ukraine as civil war follows the Bolshevik Revolution

1922 British census shows Jews make up eleven per cent of the population in Palestine

THE TWICE PROMISED LAND

The 19th-century Zionists could hardly have chosen a worse moment to begin migrating to Palestine. It had become part of the Ottoman Empire, and just as the first modern Zionists were arriving, the Arabs there were trying to shake off colonial rule. Should the Jews have their homeland or should the Arabs have their freedom? In the space of just a few years, Britain promised both...

THE ARAB AMBITION

At the end of the 19th century, much of the world was divided into great empires. The Ottoman Turks had founded theirs over 400 years earlier, by defeating the Byzantine Empire (the Christian successor to the Roman Empire). But when the Zionist project was getting under way, the Ottoman Empire was a shadow of its former self, and the Arabs of Palestine were dreaming of independence. The following years would change the regional power structure beyond all recognition.

THE ARAB DEAL

World War I began the change. The Ottoman Turks became enemies of Britain and France - then two of the biggest imperial powers - and so the British devised a plan to attack the Turks in their own backyard. In a series of letters between the British High Commissioner in Egypt, Sir Henry McMahon, and the Arab ruler of Mecca, Sharif Hussein, Britain promised to help create an independent Arab state in return for assistance in overthrowing the Turks.

In 1916, the Arabs rose up against their colonial overlords. They looked forward to the kind of post-war self-determination that was being proposed for the populations of European empires by American President Woodrow Wilson.

British Colonel TE Lawrence (here shown in Arab dress) helped lead the Arab revolt of 1916.

'Great Britain is prepared to recognise and uphold the independence of the Arabs in all the regions lying within the frontiers proposed by the Sharif of Mecca.'

Letter from Sir Henry McMahon to Sharif Hussein, 24 October 1915

A PROMISE TO THE JEWS

The Arabs in Palestine were to be sorely disappointed. During the final year of World War I, Britain's Foreign Secretary, Arthur Balfour, published a letter he had written to a prominent British Zionist, Lord Rothschild. In it, he announced his government's support for a Jewish homeland in Palestine, so long as this did not infringe the rights of non-Jews there.

The Balfour Declaration, as it has become known, may have been a war strategy, just like the McMahon-Hussein letters. Britain probably hoped to encourage loyalty among Jews who lived in the countries of its enemies, Germany and Austria-Hungary. It is

> '**His Majesty's Government views with favour the establishment in Palestine of a national home for the Jewish people, and will use their best endeavours to facilitate the achievement of this object, it being clearly understood that nothing shall be done which may prejudice the existing civil and religious rights of existing non-Jewish communities in Palestine.**'
>
> **The Balfour Declaration, November 1917**

also possible that Britain wanted a larger Jewish population in the Middle East to block any French imperial expansion after World War I. The Palestinians rejected the Declaration.

A BLURRED MESSAGE

The Balfour Declaration opened the door for the first time to officially sanctioned Jewish migration to Palestine. However, it did not specify where Palestine began and ended, nor what limits the proposed homeland might have. For his part, McMahon did not even mention Palestine, though Arabs assumed it was included in his offer of independence. These ambiguities would have serious repercussions in later years, as Jews and Arabs fought for control of the territory.

Arthur Balfour, 1917.

| **WORLD WAR I** | **June 1913** First Arab National Congress convened in Paris; calls for Arab autonomy within the Ottoman Empire | **4 August 1914** Outbreak of World War I

14 July 1915 McMahon-Hussein correspondence starts; Britain | promises Arab independence in return for help in overthrowing Ottoman Turks

2 November 1917 Balfour Declaration | promises Jewish homeland in Palestine

31 October 1918 Ottoman Turks defeated in World War I |

During World War I, Britain gained the former Ottoman territory of Palestine. After the war, the League of Nations was formed – an international forum to prevent future conflicts. Because Britain favoured the idea of a Jewish homeland in Palestine, the League granted it a mandate to govern the territory, hoping that this would lead to a smooth handover of power to the Jews. In fact, it would lead to a relentless escalation of violence.

JEWISH PIONEERS

In 1919, the future Israeli president, Chaim Weizmann (1874-1952), and Emir Feisal (1883-1933) - son of Hussein of Mecca - agreed to co-operate to establish both Jewish and Arab independence in Palestine. But as the ·Palestinian population opposed a Jewish homeland on their territory, this 'two-state' solution was soon replaced by a struggle to control all of Palestine. Due to British incentives, the number of Jews arriving there increased rapidly in the 1920s and 1930s.

Emir Feisal supported a 'two-state' Palestine.

In order to lay claim to Palestine, the Jews had somehow to out-populate the Arab majority. They began by purchasing Arab land. Although this was perfectly legal, it was resented by many Palestinians because the deals were often made with wealthy Arabs who were absentee landlords, and this left their tenant farmers without a livelihood. Arab protests soon gave way to violence.

THE 'FIRST PARTITION'

In 1921-22 Winston Churchill, who was then British Colonial Secretary, arranged an extension of the British mandate to the parts of Palestine that lay east of the River Jordan. The new territory was not subject to the Balfour Declaration, but was placed under the nominal rule of Abdullah - another son of Hussein of Mecca - and became known as Transjordan. Churchill's action avoided an attack by Abdullah upon French-controlled Syria, and did not meet with any resistance from the League of Nations. However, in the original mandated region, it was met with fury. Jews and Palestinian Arabs alike began to speak of an illegal 'partition' of Palestine. Each group claimed that a large part of its would-be homeland had been stolen, in order to appease Abdullah. Some Israelis have since used the idea that Transjordan belongs to Palestine to argue that the Palestinians should make their permanent home in the modern state of Jordan.

GUERRILLA WARFARE

A number of Jewish militias emerged in the struggle for Palestine: Haganah – formed in 1920 in response to Arab attacks – was one of several self-defence forces, and developed into a substantial military body that was later the basis for the Israel Defence Forces. Irgun was formed by a group of extremist Haganah members, and carried out reprisals against the Palestinians. Lehi, also known as the Stern Gang, concentrated mainly on attacking the British, whom it saw as illegal occupiers of Palestine. Irgun and Lehi were responsible for a notorious massacre of civilians in the Palestinian village of Deir Yassin in 1948.

Not much remained of the King David Hotel after it was blown up by Irgun in July 1946 (see page 16).

VIOLENCE AND COUNTER-VIOLENCE

As the British mandate continued, all efforts to stem the violence between Arabs and Jews were in vain. Britain offered to give the Palestinians a legislative council if they accepted the Balfour Declaration, but they refused, as it would have meant allowing the Jews to divide their land. The result was that, while the Jews became more organised, the Palestinians lacked a political forum.

The continued refusal to share communities and institutions further alienated the two peoples from one another. By the 1930s the situation was desperate. Amid strikes, riots and inter-communal massacres, Britain proposed a formal partition of Palestine. When the Palestinians rejected this, London imposed a clampdown on Jewish immigration. Now, the Zionists were outraged. In 1940, Abraham Stern founded the Stern Gang, an underground militia that aimed to achieve a Jewish state in all of Palestine - including Transjordan - by attacking the British themselves.

PALESTINE UNDER THE BRITISH

25 April 1920 Britain given control over Palestine

15 June 1920 Haganah defence militia is formed

11 April 1921 East Palestine becomes Transjordan

23 August 1929 Rioting in Palestine; hundreds of deaths

1936-9 Arabs stage general strike

7 July 1937 British Peel Commission recommends Arab/ Jewish partition

17 May 1939 Britain restricts Jewish migration

3 September 1939 World War II begins

17 July 1940 Irgun splits over anti-British activities; Stern Gang formed

6 November 1944 Stern Gang assassinates British Middle East minister, Lord Moyne, in Egypt

22 July 1946 Irgun guerrillas bomb the King David Hotel in Jerusalem

STATEHOOD DECLARED

World War II left Britain a weaker international power, and less willing to bear the cost of unrest in Palestine. The war also revealed Hitler's unimaginable brutality towards Jews, adding to the clamour for Jewish statehood. When events reached their climax in 1948, the Arabs were the losers.

BRITISH HUMILIATION

As Nazi Germany crumbled in 1945, the dreadful crimes of Hitler's regime were uncovered: some six million Jews were among the victims of a deliberate extermination campaign. Now, the need for a homeland for Jews assumed a new urgency.

Meanwhile, Britain was at the end of its tether over Palestine: Arabs killed Jews, Jews killed Arabs, and both had attacked British forces. In 1946, the Zionist guerrilla group, Irgun, bombed British military headquarters at the King David Hotel in Jerusalem. The incident, which killed ninety-one people, symbolised London's weakness, and in April 1947 the government announced its intention to hand over Palestine to the League of Nations' successor, the United Nations (UN).

A PLAN FOR PARTITION

In November 1947, as Britain was preparing to leave Palestine, the UN came up with another partition scheme. The plan gave the Jews their own state, based on the areas where they had purchased the most land. Arabs would control much of the remaining territory. Yet another part of the land, which included Jerusalem, would be given international status. Eventually, the Jews supported the idea, though Palestinians still opposed the division of their land.

A group of Jewish children, survivors of the Nazis' Auschwitz death camp, 1945.

STATEHOOD PROCLAIMED

In the last, chaotic months of British rule, the Zionists sensed an historic opportunity. They used this time to seize all the land assigned to them under the UN plan, and more besides. As they did so, they forced many Arabs to flee from their homes. Up to half a million Palestinian refugees were created between April 1947 and May 1948, when the last British troops left. On 15 May 1948, as soon as the British mandate had expired, the Zionists proclaimed a new state in the areas of Palestine under Jewish control. *Eretz-Isreal* (land of Israel) was born. Palestinians still refer to that moment as *al-Nakba* (the catastrophe).

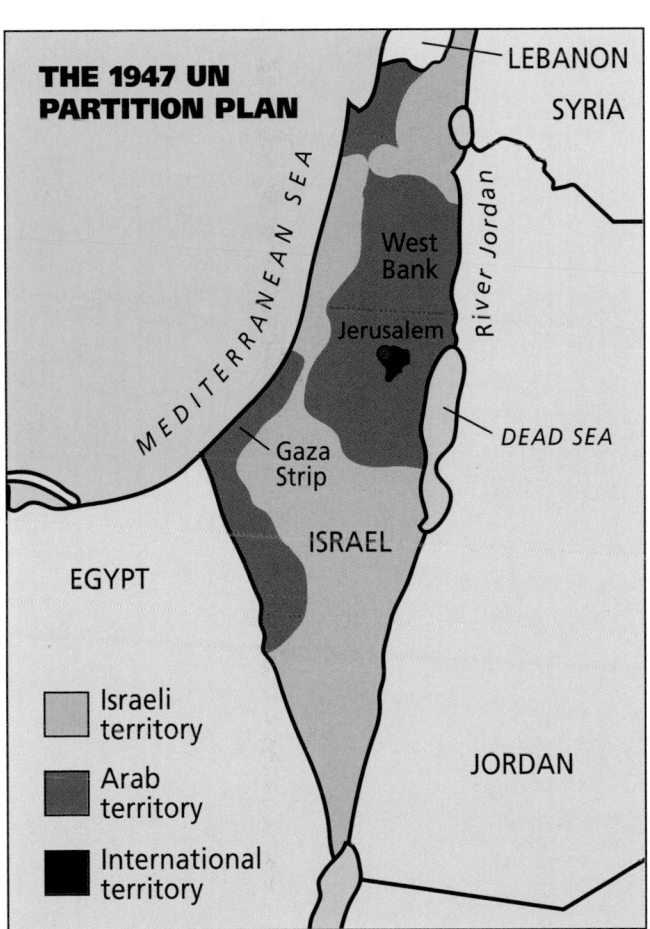

THE 1947 UN PARTITION PLAN

LEBANON
SYRIA
MEDITERRANEAN SEA
West Bank
River Jordan
Jerusalem
DEAD SEA
Gaza Strip
ISRAEL
EGYPT
JORDAN

- ☐ Israeli territory
- ▨ Arab territory
- ■ International territory

DAVID BEN-GURION (1886–1973)

Israelis consider David Ben-Gurion to be the father of their nation. Born in Poland, he was one of the socialist pioneers who emigrated to Palestine at the turn of the 20th century. Soon afterwards, he formed one of the Jewish self-defence militias, and led the Jewish workers' party, Mapai. He read the proclamation of state in 1948, and became Israel's first prime minister until 1953, and also between 1955 and 1963. After his retirement he became a symbolic figurehead of the Jewish state.

THE BIRTH OF ISRAEL

2 April 1947 Britain announces it will hand over Palestine to United Nations

15 May 1947 UN sets up a committee on Palestine

29 November 1947 United Nations Resolution 181 recommends partition

18 July 1947 Refugee ship *Exodus,* carrying Jewish survivors of Nazi brutality, is refused entry to Palestine by Britain, which deports them; the anger this incident creates shores up support for a Jewish state

25 March 1948 US President Harry Truman announces his support for partition

9 April 1948 Deir Yassin massacre: scores of Palestinian civilians killed in joint Lehi/Irgun offensive

April-May 1948 Jewish victories over the Arabs in West Jerusalem, Jaffa and Safed

14 May 1948 David Ben-Gurion proclaims the state of Israel, to come into force on 15 May 1948 as the last British troops pull out

BORN UNDER PUNCHES

The birth of Israel in 1948 signalled a new idealism among Jews. At last, after centuries of persecution, they looked towards the protection and dignity of statehood. Few could have known that this would begin half-a-century of conflict.

VIOLENT REACTION

The new state of Israel was quickly recognised by both America and the Soviet Union. The local reception, though equally swift, was less favourable. As soon as statehood was declared, the Arab states of Egypt, Syria, Jordan, Iraq and Lebanon invaded on behalf of the Palestinians, beginning what the Israelis call their 'War of Independence'. Initially, the Arabs made some gains. Ultimately, however, they were badly co-ordinated and proved no match for the highly motivated Jewish defenders. The Israelis secured access to West Jerusalem and held on to it, defeated Syrian and Iraqi forces, and repelled an Egyptian advance across the Negev Desert. Indeed, they ended the war with even more land than before - seventy-five per cent of former British Palestine.

Israel's enemies fight in the Battle for the Negev, 1948.

THE POST-WAR LANDSCAPE

1948 was even more of a disaster for the Palestinians themselves. Once again, they had to flee as the Israelis made their counter-attacks. Jerusalem - far from being set aside as a special international zone - was left divided between Israel and Jordan. The Jordanians annexed their half of the city, along with most of what was left of Palestine - namely, the West Bank of the River Jordan. Many Palestinian refugees set up home in this region in vast camps. Others went as far away as Lebanon and Syria. Their departure was valuable to Israel, for it meant the new state had a Jewish majority. So, when Palestinians demanded the right to go home after the war, Israel's leader, David Ben-Gurion, refused. In turn, Jews living in Arab countries now found themselves at greater risk. Many left for Israel, where they were joined by others from further afield, including survivors of the Nazi genocide in Europe.

> **'A miraculous clearing of the land: the miraculous simplification of Israel's task.'**
>
> **Israel's first president, Chaim Weizmann, speaking about the flight of Arab refugees, 1948**

BITTER LEGACY

The Arab states were beaten, but still refused to recognise Israel, vowing to fight another day. Not only did they believe the

Palestinians had been wronged in 1948; they also feared for their own territory. As if to confirm their suspicions, Israel declared West Jerusalem its capital in 1949. Palestinian rage had been matched by Israeli determination. The Arab-Israeli conflict as we know it had begun.

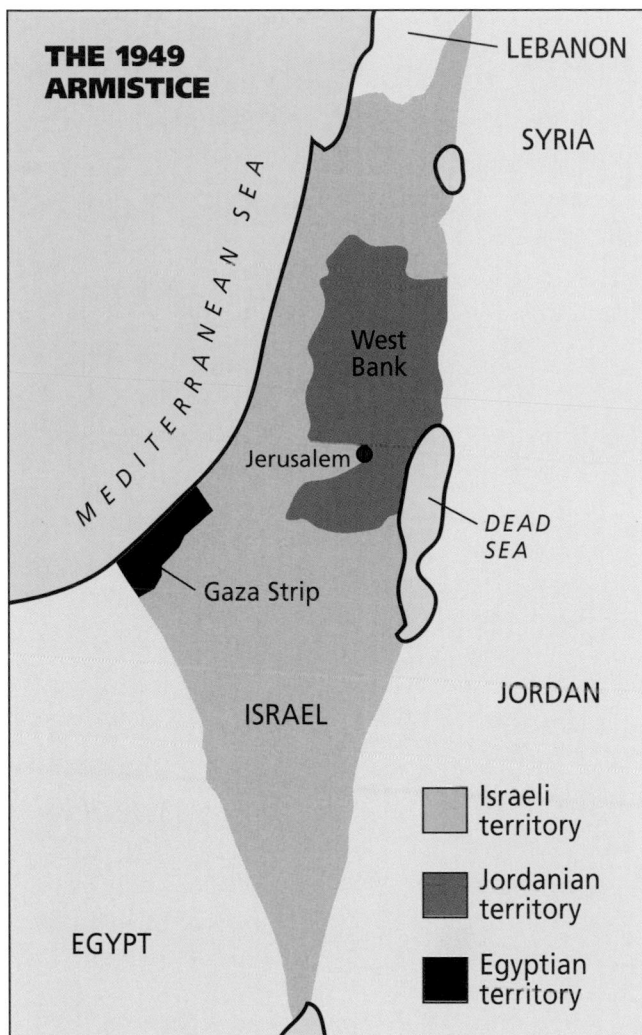

THE 1949 ARMISTICE

LEBANON

SYRIA

MEDITERRANEAN SEA

West Bank

Jerusalem

DEAD SEA

Gaza Strip

JORDAN

ISRAEL

EGYPT

Israeli territory

Jordanian territory

Egyptian territory

MOSHE DAYAN (1915-81)

One of a generation of Jewish leaders who fought to establish their nation, Moshe Dayan was imprisoned under the British mandate for co-founding Haganah. He was later freed to fight alongside British forces in World War II, and lost an eye doing so; thereafter he wore an eye-patch. He distinguished himself in the 1948 'War of Independence', and was Chief of Staff in the Suez campaign of 1956. Then he entered politics. As Defence Minister he masterminded Israel's very swift victory over the Arabs in 1967. In the 1970s, Dayan was criticised over Arab gains in the Yom Kippur War. He resigned from Menachem Begin's government in 1979 over its lack of progress towards an accord with the Palestinians.

THE FIRST ARAB-ISRAELI WAR

15 May 1948 Arab armies enter Palestine and Israel

25 May 1948 Arabs repel Israeli Defence Forces at Latrun

11 June 1948 First truce, mediated by UN

9 July 1948 Fighting breaks out again

17 September 1948 Stern Gang murders the Swedish UN mediator, Count Folke Bernadotte

29 November 1948 Israel makes its first application to join UN; it is unsuccessful

11 December 1948 UN Resolution 194

proclaims the right of Palestinian refugees to return to their homes

7 January 1949 Ceasefire: Israel withdraws from Sinai

16 February 1949 Israel's first president, Chaim Weizmann, is sworn in

February-July 1949 Armistice agreements concluded with the various Arab states

11 May 1949 Israel admitted to United Nations

13 December 1949 Israel declares West Jerusalem its capital city

After 1948, Arab states competed with each other for the honour of representing the Palestinians. Soon, one man emerged as champion. His dream was a single Arab nation, united against the Jewish state.

AN ARAB HERO

Israel may have won the 1948 war, but border skirmishes continued into the 1950s, killing hundreds of Arabs and Jews each year. An even greater threat to the Israelis was their giant southern neighbour, Egypt. There, a coup in 1952 had deposed the king and an army colonel, Gamal Abdel Nasser, had risen to power. Nasser had fought in the 1948 war and witnessed the poor co-ordination of the various Arab armies. He believed the Arabs should unite to form one nation, which could challenge both Israel and western colonialism more effectively.

ISRAELI FEAR

Israel rightly saw Nasser as a threat, and all the more so when he succeeded in removing British troops from Egypt. The Israelis therefore tried to portray him as a danger to the outside world. The extent of their determination became clear when, in 1954, a number of attacks on British and American interests in Egypt - seemingly carried out by Egyptians - turned out to be the work of a Jewish sabotage group. The so-called Lavon Affair took its name from the subsequent resignation of Israel's Defence Minister Pinhas Lavon.

THE SUEZ CRISIS

Soon, Nasser's impact spread beyond the region. He took the Suez Canal into ownership by the Egyptian state. That meant Egypt could block foreign shipping and trade if it wished. The British saw this as a threat to their economic and military

GAMAL ABDEL NASSER (1918–70)

Nasser grew up in an Egypt that was profoundly unequal and subservient to the British. As an army officer, he formed a secret society, the Free Officers, to change things. In 1952 the Free Officers ousted Egypt's King Farouk in a *coup d'état*, and two years later, Nasser himself assumed power. His vision was secular and socialist, and included a raft of grand development schemes. A champion of the Third World, he co-founded the Non-Aligned Movement, and his nationalisation of the Suez Canal was a powerful backlash against colonialism. However, his dream of Arab unity, which reached its height with a short-lived merger between Egypt and Syria, was never to materialise.

interests. And Nasser enraged France by supporting nationalist violence against its colonists in Algeria. Thus a common interest emerged between the British and French governments and the Israelis. In 1956, they hatched a secret plot to unseat Nasser through a second Arab-Israeli war.

According to the plan, Israel was to attack Egypt and an Anglo-French force would then intervene, purporting to separate the combatants, but actually planning to attack Egypt as well. The operation began in October 1956, and met with considerable military success. However, the three allies had reckoned without one key problem: their

This 1956 view of part of Suez shows the ships sunk by Egypt to block the canal.

campaign infuriated US President Dwight Eisenhower, who was in the middle of a re-election campaign focused on the theme of peace. He demanded that they stop the military action at once, and they were forced to do so.

Britain and France both lost their status as world powers after this humiliating climbdown. But it made Nasser the hero of the Arab world. With so many Arabs backing his foreign policy, Egypt became an even more potent threat to the young Jewish state.

THE 1950s

24 April 1950 Formal annexation of West Bank to Jordan

5 July 1950 The Israeli parliament, the Knesset, adopts the Law of Return; it gives any Jew the right to live in Israel

11 August 1952 Hussein ibn Talal proclaimed king of Jordan

23 July 1952 Nasser plans a military coup in Egypt; deposes King Farouk and establishes a republic

7 December 1953 Moshe Sharett replaces David Ben-Gurion as Israel's prime minister

15 November 1954 Nasser becomes president of Egypt

2 November 1955 Ben-Gurion resumes the Israeli premiership

26 July 1956 Nasser nationalises the Suez Canal

29 October 1956 Israeli invasion of Egypt starts

5 January 1957 American President Eisenhower announces

an offer of US assistance to Middle East states threatened by communism

1 February 1958 Egypt and Syria merge as the United Arab Republic

10 October 1959 Yasser Arafat and colleagues establish Fatah (Conquest) movement

THE FRENCH CONNECTION

In its first two decades, Israel struggled to find military allies. Some of the world's great powers wanted to keep their distance from the new state; others opposed it outright. However, one country did come to its aid. The actions of France helped to create a regional superpower.

ISRAEL ALONE

Today, Israel maintains a close alliance with the United States, but this was not always the case. Initially, its appeals for military help received a cool response from Washington, because the Americans didn't want to risk upsetting the Arab countries upon whom they depended for oil. On the other hand, the Israelis could not look to the Communist bloc, for by the 1950s, the Soviet Union was beginning to arm their main adversaries, the Syrians and Egyptians. The Israeli premier, David Ben-Gurion, therefore decided that he must find a western ally to supply his country with technical and military support.

BROTHERS IN ARMS

The French, meanwhile, had their own conflict with the Arabs in the mid-1950s. A rebellion in Algeria, supported by Egypt's President Nasser, threatened to end their colonial presence there, and so, by 1956, they and the Israelis discovered that they had a common enemy. Just before the Suez Crisis in which both countries plotted to overthrow Nasser, Shimon Peres - then Director-General of the Israeli Defence Ministry - organised a secret meeting in Paris, where he cemented the Franco-Israeli friendship with a major weapons deal. The French agreed to supply modern tanks, and

Algerians protest at the French National Assembly, 9 March 1956.

their very latest jet fighter, the 'Mystère'. In the years that followed, the French became Israel's chief armourer.

French Prime Minister Guy Mollet shown speaking on the radio during the 1956 Algerian crisis.

ISRAEL GETS THE BOMB

The failure of the Suez operation did little to spoil the accord. Indeed, just a year or so afterwards, France put Israel on the nuclear road. The French prime minister, Guy Mollet, was quoted as saying privately that he owed Israel his nuclear co-operation because of the failure of Suez. Ben-Gurion saw nuclear weapons as a great practical asset; they vastly increased Israel's military potential in any conflict. Moreover, he reasoned, Israel's possession of them might be an incentive for the Arabs to make peace.

Again, Shimon Peres supervised the project, which saw French engineers helping to build a top-secret atomic reactor at Dimona in the Negev Desert. This was in direct contravention of United States' efforts to prevent nuclear proliferation. Israel has never publicly admitted its nuclear capability. Nevertheless, rumours of its nuclear potential have undoubtedly influenced the decisions of its enemies.

> '**We shall never again be led as lambs to the slaughter.**'
>
> **Ernst David Bergmann, chairman of the Israel Atomic Energy Commission (IAEC)**

THE END OF THE AFFAIR

The curious alliance between Israel and France ended thanks in part to the same crisis that began it. In 1958, Charles de Gaulle became French president, and surprised his followers by announcing a withdrawal from Algeria. The Algerian war of independence ended with the Evian Treaty in 1962, and allowed Paris to resume links with the Arab world. The special relationship between the two nations gradually cooled. Later on, de Gaulle referred to the Jews as a 'domineering' people, which caused uproar in Israel. But by then, the Israelis had the modern weapons they needed, and in future would prove capable of resisting the hostility of Arab states.

ISRAEL AND FRANCE

1 November 1954 Algerian insurgency begins, supported by Nasser

June 1956 Shimon Peres convenes a secret arms meeting with the French in

the run-up to the joint Suez operation

21 December 1958 Charles de Gaulle is elected president of France

5 July 1962 Algeria declares its independence from France

30 September 1986 Former Israeli technician, Mordechai Vanunu,

is captured by Mossad agents in Rome after leaking details of Israel's nuclear programme to a London newspaper; Vanunu jailed for 18 years

THE SIX-DAY WAR

As the 1960s wore on, tension between Israel and her neighbours remained at fever pitch, and a third war seemed inevitable. When it came, it was short, sharp and decisive.

BUILD-UP TO WAR

After Suez, the Egyptian Sinai region bordering Israel became home to United Nations peacekeepers. This had been on Ben-Gurion's insistence but, since the peacekeepers did not encroach on any Jewish land, it angered the Egyptians. Tension was also high over an Israeli scheme to take more water from the River Jordan, over Syrian help for Palestinian *fedayeen* (resistance fighters), and because of continued Arab hostility to the Jewish state in general. Nasser forged defence pacts with Syria, Jordan and Iraq, and in 1967 he got rid of the UN peacekeepers and began a blockade of Israeli shipping in the Gulf of Aqaba, to the south of Israel. The Israeli Knesset declared this an act of aggression.

LIGHTNING STRIKES

Israel did not wait for an Arab attack before opening fire itself. Instead, it applied a strategy of pre-emptive military action that stunned the world. In a single operation on 5 June 1967, Israeli planes destroyed almost the entire Egyptian air force before it had even got off the ground. The next day, Israel's army started picking off one front after another, defeating first the Egyptians, then Jordan and finally Syria.

The Arabs were divided over their war aims, and the Israelis found little co-ordinated resistance. They captured the West Bank of the River Jordan; they captured the Golan Heights overlooking the Syrian-Israeli border; they captured the Gaza Strip from Egypt - and the entire Sinai peninsula up to the Suez

THE SIX-DAY WAR

☐ Territory captured by Israel

MEDITERRANEAN SEA

SYRIA

Golan Heights

River Jordan

West Bank

Gaza Strip

Jerusalem

DEAD SEA

ISRAEL

EGYPT

JORDAN

Suez Canal

Sinai Peninsula

Canal. Most significantly of all, they captured the whole of Jerusalem.

The speed and scale of events left the Arab states aghast. Another 300,000 Palestinians were displaced from their homes, and the territory in Israeli hands almost tripled overnight - a devastating humiliation, especially for Nasser, who offered his resignation in response. Moreover, East Jerusalem, containing some of Islam's holiest places, was now under Jewish control. Muslims had not been forced to relinquish

> **'I am ready to bear the whole responsibility.'**
>
> **from Nasser's resignation speech, 9 June 1967**

Israeli forces watch enemy movements during the Six-Day War, 1967.

the city since the crusades, over eight centuries earlier - a parallel not lost on their outraged leaders. To Israel, the gains were equally momentous, since they gave Jews access to some of their own most prized religious sites, and appeared to represent a valuable bargaining chip for peace.

RESOLUTION 242

In November 1967, the United Nations Security Council passed Resolution 242, which called on Israel to withdraw from the territories it had occupied, in return for Arab recognition of its sovereignty and security.

Since then, the resolution has frequently been cited by Israel's critics, who point out that the most important territory captured in 1967 has remained under Israeli occupation. In reply, Israel has argued that its enemies have no intention of guaranteeing peace. In 1980, Israel declared all of Jerusalem to be its eternal capital.

January-April Border skirmishes and air battles between Israel and Syria raise tension and expectation of war

15-18 May Nasser asks UN Emergency Force between Israel and Egypt to leave

May Egypt closes the Straits of Tiran to Israeli shipping

5th June War breaks out: Israeli air force destroys most Egyptian planes on the ground in a pre-emptive strike

7 June Jordan cedes the West Bank and East Jerusalem to the Israeli Defence Forces

8 June Israel accidentally hits US observer ship, *Liberty*, killing 34 crew

10 June Israel takes strategic Golan Heights from Syria, removing a vantage point from which the Syrians had been able to fire

August-September Khartoum Arab Summit, at which the Arab states declare their refusal to recognise, negotiate or be reconciled with Israel

22 November UN Security Council passes Resolution 242

SETTLEMENTS

The territorial advances of 1967 gave Israel what some Zionists had always wanted – free rein to colonise all of Palestine west of the River Jordan. Now, a new and intractable element would be introduced into the Middle East conflict.

THE ALLON PLAN

Soon after the Six-Day War ended, Israel decided to capitalise on its new acquisitions. One of its greatest strategists, a minister called Yigal Allon, suggested using the Occupied Territories to create secure borders with the Arab world. He proposed annexing those parts of the territories with the biggest defence potential, including the Jordan River valley and greater Jerusalem. The remainder, around sixty per cent of the captured land, would be returned to the Arabs and form an autonomous Palestinian state, politically linked to Jordan although surrounded by Israeli territory.

Despite Arab governments comprehensively rejecting the Allon Plan, the Israelis went

ahead according to its principles. Over the next ten years, the government built military settlements across the areas of proposed annexation, while avoiding the remaining occupied land.

RELIGIOUS FERVOUR

The government's defensive settlements were not the end of the matter, however. East Jerusalem's seizure in 1967 had inspired a number of messianic Jewish cults, which gave rise to a movement called *Gush Emunim* (Bloc of the Faithful). Under its leader, the militant rabbi, Moshe Levinger, a group of activists occupied a site in Hebron - within the area earmarked for Palestinian autonomy - and refused to leave. In the end, the Israeli government gave in to them, and they established the town of Kiryat Arba. Their tactics were then copied by others bent on taking all of Palestine for religious reasons, and Jewish communities sprang up throughout the West Bank and elsewhere. These settlers often refer to the Occupied Territories by their Biblical names.

FAIT ACCOMPLI

After 1977, the nature and the pace of settlement activity changed. For the first time in Israel's history, the right-wing Likud Party formed a government. Now the state, too, focused on recreating the Greater Israel of Biblical times. The new prime minister, Menachem Begin, made it his policy to turn settlements into irreversible 'facts on the ground' to encourage the Occupied Territories' permanent incorporation into

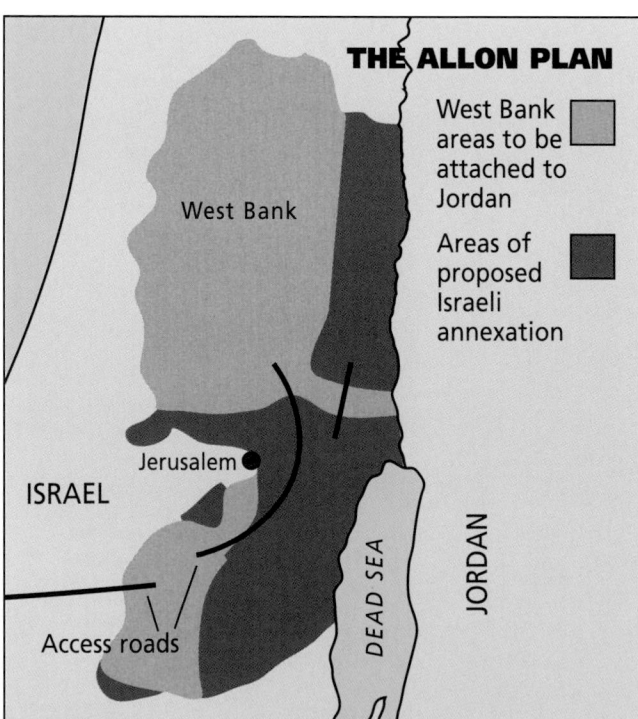

THE ALLON PLAN

West Bank areas to be attached to Jordan

Areas of proposed Israeli annexation

West Bank

Jerusalem

ISRAEL

JORDAN

DEAD SEA

Access roads

KING HUSSEIN (1935-99)

Most settlements are on former Jordanian territory, and over half of all Jordanians are refugees; yet King Hussein of Jordan always remained a moderate fighter on behalf of the Palestinian cause. After 1967, he concluded that the Occupied Territories could never be recovered by force, and set about the near-impossible task of trying to reconcile Arab opinion with the outside world. Educated in Britain and the Middle East, he was uniquely placed to do this, though it earned him the hostility of militants. The king played a key role in the Oslo Peace accord of 1993, before his death from cancer six years later.

Israel. The government offered financial incentives for Jews to move to new housing projects, and the number of those doing so mushroomed. In the 1990s, the then Housing Minister, Ariel Sharon, presided over another huge settlement drive, openly admitting that his aim was to make a Palestinian state in the Occupied Territories much more difficult to achieve.

NO SURRENDER

Settlements in the Occupied Territories have been declared illegal under international law, and there have been calls for Israel to dismantle them. Yet, at the start of the 21st century, around 150 remained outside the pre-1967 green-line border between Israel and the West Bank, with more than 200,000 Jewish settlers

living in them. Some settlers are inspired by religion, others simply by the prospect of cheaper and more spacious housing.

The settlements have divided and encroached upon Palestinian property, and they have been the targets of repeated Arab attacks. Yet settlers are determined to stay put, and their presence has become one of the most difficult issues facing the region.

> **'I don't think there is any greater obstacle to peace than settlement activity.'**
>
> **American Secretary of State, James Baker, 22 May 1991**

SETTLEMENTS

26 July 1967 Presentation of Allon Plan

4 April 1968 Rabbi Moshe Levinger and his supporters celebrate Passover in Hebron, later refusing to leave and paving the way for further settlements

17 May 1977 Israeli elections; Likud forces the Labour Party into opposition for the first time. Menachem Begin becomes Prime Minister

22 March 1979 UN Security Council Resolution 446 demands that Israel dismantle settlements

30 July 1980 Israel declares all of Jerusalem to be its undivided and eternal capital

January 1990 Jews begin leaving the Soviet Union to live in Israel. Israeli premier Yitzhak Shamir vows to find homes for all who migrate

The humiliation of the Six-Day War was a rude awakening for the Palestinians. It shattered their belief that liberation could be achieved by the intervention of neighbouring Arab states. Now, they had to take matters into their own hands.

A CALL FOR ACTION

The Palestine Liberation Organisation (PLO) was formed in 1964 by a summit of Arab governments. It was originally little more than a device to protect Nasser's power, which was threatened by demands for more action against Israel. However, the defeat of 1967 left Nasser and his pan-Arab theories completely discredited and this encouraged a takeover of the PLO by more radical elements. As the 1960s drew to a close, the world was introduced to PLO guerrilla warfare. Bombs and aircraft hijackings were now the order of the day.

THE RISE OF FATAH

Yasser Arafat's Fatah militia was founded in the 1950s, but only became active as a guerrilla force in 1965. Its prestige was vastly enhanced three years later, when the Israelis attacked its headquarters in the Jordanian village of Karameh. Although the Israeli mission succeeded, Fatah commandos and their allies managed to inflict substantial casualties. Thereafter, Fatah went from strength to strength, gaining more recruits and winning more influence among the Palestinians. In 1969, it became the dominant faction within the PLO after Arafat was elected as chairman of the organisation.

BLACK SEPTEMBER

Despite its popularity among disaffected Palestinians, the PLO has had a mixed relationship with Arab governments - supported by some, and viewed with

YASSER ARAFAT (1929-)

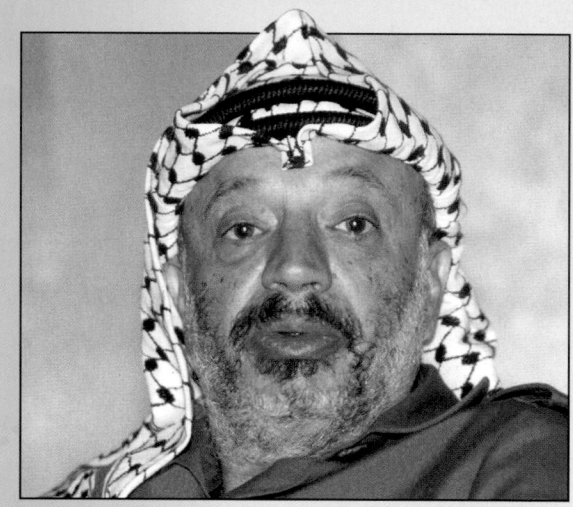

Yasser Arafat was brought up in 1930s' Jerusalem, amid early Arab-Jewish violence. Later, as a student in Cairo, he co-founded the Fatah guerrilla faction. After decades of violence, Arafat's decision to make peace with Israel won him the Nobel Peace Prize in 1994, along with Yitzhak Rabin and Shimon Peres. However, his subsequent leadership of the autonomous Palestinian Authority was marred by accusations of despotism. Arafat alienated many of his allies. His inability to tackle militants on his own side made him, as far as Israel was concerned, an obstacle to a lasting peace.

suspicion by others. By the time of Fatah's takeover of the PLO a crisis was already looming in Jordan, from where the PLO was mounting raids on Israel: the PLO's strength had made it a rival to King Hussein's government. In addition, Israel was threatening Jordan with retaliation for

A scene of grief as the body of an Israeli athlete arrives home from the 1972 Munich Olympic Games.

the incursions. So, in 1970, the king banned PLO activity on his territory, and fighting soon broke out between his army and the guerrillas.

In September 1970, one of the most radical PLO factions, the Popular Front for the Liberation of Palestine (PFLP), increased the tension by hijacking three airliners and flying them to Jordan. This was the last straw for King Hussein. He ordered his troops to evict the PLO. In the conflict that followed, some 3,000 Palestinians were killed. Black September, as it became known, gave its name to a PLO splinter

group, which later assassinated the Jordanian prime minister. Black September terrorists were also responsible for the deaths of 11 Israeli athletes at the 1972 Munich Olympic Games.

INTERNATIONAL RECOGNITION

Although PLO violence continued, Yasser Arafat believed that attacks like those of Black September damaged his cause. He attempted to rein in the extremists. Arab governments were sufficiently impressed to recognise the PLO as the 'sole legitimate representative of the Palestinian people'. Eventually, the international community seemed to agree: in 1974, Arafat went on to address the United Nations, where the PLO was given observer status.

THE PLO

2 June 1964
Foundation of the PLO

1 January 1965
First Fatah operation

11 December 1967
PFLP formed

1-4 February 1969 Yasser Arafat and Fatah gain control of PLO

10 February 1970 King Hussein issues decrees against PLO activity

6 September 1970 PFLP hijack four airliners

17-27 September 1970 Black September: King Hussein's troops move against PLO

28 November 1971 Black September group murder Jordanian Prime Minister, Wasfi al-Tal

5 September 1972 Attack on Israeli Olympic athletes

26-29 October 1974 Arab League recognises PLO as representative of Palestinian people

13 November 1974 Yasser Arafat addresses UN; invites the world to choose between war and peace

At the same time as Palestinian guerrilla violence was increasing, the two most powerful Arab states tried once again to defeat Israel. Unable to recover their 1967 losses by diplomacy, six years later Egypt and Syria staged a surprise attack.

RAPID ADVANCES

The Yom Kippur War - also known as the Ramadan or October War - was the brainchild of Egypt's president and Nasser's successor, Anwar Sadat. He hoped it would force the United States to help him recover Egyptian land occupied by Israel. So, on 6 October 1973, Egypt and Syria (with support from other Arab countries), caught the Israelis off guard as they celebrated the festival of Yom Kippur, one of the holiest times in the Jewish calendar. The Arabs stole a march on their enemy, which they also vastly outnumbered, and made rapid gains in both the north and south. To begin with, things looked very bleak for Israel.

SUPERPOWER INFLUENCE

As the war progressed, superpower assistance played an important role on both sides. Egypt and Syria were using Soviet weapons, and it was American assistance that finally enabled the Israelis to counter-attack. A month-long airlift entitled Operation Nickel Grass gave them vital arms supplies. Washington also passed on intelligence from

Israeli 155mm guns bombard Syrian positions during the Yom Kippur War, 1973.

American spy planes, which allowed the Israelis to identify Arab troop formations and deploy their forces more effectively. As a result, the tide turned against the Arabs. In fact, the Israelis extended their post-1967 borders, even setting up a bridgehead on the west bank of the Suez Canal, and coming within fifty kilometres of the Syrian capital, Damascus. However, when the Soviets and Americans saw that the conflict might escalate into a war between themselves, they quickly separated the two sides.

ANWAR SADAT (1918-81)

Originally one of the plotters who deposed King Farouk, Sadat became president of Egypt on Nasser's death in 1970. Despite losing the October War of 1973, he turned this into a moral victory. Still, he longed to end Egypt's burden as the Arabs' main protagonist against Israel. A ruthless politician, Sadat also turned his country away from Moscow and towards the United States, and he finally drew a line under Nasser's pan-Arabism.

MIXED CONSEQUENCES

The war ended after three weeks with a ceasefire brokered through the United Nations. UN Resolution 338 called on both sides to end the war, to implement Resolution 242 in full, and to negotiate a just peace in the region. This paved the way for a later agreement between Israel and Egypt. However, Israel became more diplomatically isolated. The Arabs and their Soviet backers

persuaded many developing countries to sever links with Israel. In 1975, a resolution of the UN General Assembly equated Zionism with racism, though this was later revoked.

THE OIL CRISIS

The October War also increased the impact of the Arab-Israeli conflict upon the outside world. Once Israel's counter-attack was under way, Arab countries belonging to the Organisation of Petroleum-Exporting Countries (OPEC) mounted an embargo against the United States and other states accused of supporting Israel. The supply of oil to world markets was cut back, leading to a fourfold increase in prices. This enormously increased the wealth of producers like Saudi Arabia, but the West was to suffer a long and painful economic downturn as a result.

The 1973 oil crisis produced huge queues and high prices at petrol stations all around the world.

THE 1973 WAR

6 October Syrian-Egyptian joint attack on Israel; PLO joins in with attacks from Lebanon

14 October America

begins Operation Nickel Grass, a crucial weapons airlift to Israel

22 October UN passes Security Council Resolution 338

11 November Israeli-Egyptian ceasefire signed: losses estimated at 8,500 Syrians and Egyptians and 6,000 Israelis

January-May 1974 Military disengagements take place between the combatants

31

AN OLIVE BRANCH FROM EGYPT

The oil crisis following 1973 brought enormous wealth to some parts of the Middle East, but in Egypt the economy faltered. If President Sadat was to win the international investment his country so badly needed, he would have to swallow his pride and make peace with the Arabs' most detested enemy.

INFITAH

After the optimism of Nasser's age, Egypt faced a variety of economic and political difficulties. The old centralised economy was not a great success, and President Sadat believed that private enterprise was needed in order to prosper. At the same time, he was painfully aware that Egyptian land, including its Sinai oilfields, remained under Israeli occupation following the October War of 1973. These problems became the twin catalysts for a new policy known as *infitah* (the open door), which ended Nasserite economic planning and allowed a foreign, private sector to develop. Sadat hoped that, by doing this, he would also win American support to recoup the lost territories.

CAMP DAVID

The Americans were keen to encourage Sadat, whom they saw as an Arab moderate, and they reacted positively to his initiative. Israel, by now battling with the PLO, was also ready to respond. The breakthrough came in 1977: Sadat used the prestige of his early victories in the October War to try and rally support for an extraordinary venture. On 19 November 1977, he flew to Jerusalem and addressed the Knesset (Israeli parliament), offering full recognition of Israel in exchange for the return of Egyptian land captured in the war. It was the first time any Arab government had acknowledged Israel's right to exist.

MENACHEM BEGIN (1913-92), TOUGH PEACEMAKER

An active Zionist from Brest-Litovsk, Poland, Begin fled his native land in 1939 after the Nazis invaded, and ended up in British Palestine as part of the Free Polish Army. After being discharged, he achieved notoriety as Commander-in-Chief of the Irgun militia. Later, he founded the Herut Freedom Movement - the basis for the nationalist Likud Party. The first Likud prime minister of Israel between 1977 and 1983, Begin expanded Jewish settlements and remained a hardline leader, despite making peace with Egypt, for which he was jointly awarded the Nobel Peace Prize.

The next year, under the mediation of a keen peacemaker - US President Jimmy Carter - Sadat and the Israeli premier, Menachem Begin, signed the historic Camp David Accord, which established normal diplomatic relations.

> *'I have not consulted as far as this decision is concerned with any of my colleagues or brothers, the Arab heads of state or the confrontation states.'*
>
> **Anwar Sadat's address to the Knesset, 20 November 1977**

An historic moment – from left, Sadat, Carter and Begin sign the Camp David Accord, 1978.

A COSTLY PRICE

After Camp David, Sadat shared the 1978 Nobel Peace Prize with Begin. However, the rest of the Arab world saw him as a traitor. The other Arab states broke diplomatic links with Egypt, imposed sanctions and expelled Cairo from the Arab League. Then, in 1981, when he was at a ceremony to mark the anniversary of the October War, Anwar Sadat was attacked by soldiers from his own army, and shot dead.

> **'We [...] witness tonight a significant achievement in the cause of peace; an achievement none thought possible a year ago, or even a month ago.'**
>
> **American President, Jimmy Carter, on the signing of the Camp David Accord, 17 September 1978**

EGYPT'S QUEST FOR PEACE

5 June 1975 Suez Canal reopens to foreign shipping after eight years

1 September 1975 'Sinai II': Israel and Egypt's treaty of disengagement

17 May 1977 Menachem Begin wins Israeli elections; formation of first non-Labour government in Israel

19 November 1977 Sadat's ground-breaking speech to the Israeli Knesset, which acknowledges Israel as a state

17 September 1978 Israel and Egypt sign Camp David Accord

6 October 1981 Anwar Sadat assassinated by militants at a military parade

26 April 1982 Israel completes withdrawal from most of the Sinai region in Egypt

LEBANON

As Egypt was making its peace with Israel, Palestinian guerrillas continued their fight with renewed vigour. The battleground now moved north to Lebanon, where it would radicalise an entire generation, and help to tear that country apart.

CIVIL WAR CHAOS

After Yasser Arafat's PLO was expelled from Jordan in 1970, it moved to Lebanon. Its presence there added to the complex power struggles that erupted in civil war five years later. The near anarchy spawned by that conflict made Lebanon an ideal base for armed militancy against neighbouring Israel. However, after making peace with Egypt in the south, the Israelis were free to move against the PLO in the north. In 1978, they invaded Lebanon. Operation Litani involved 20,000 troops. The PLO remained in Lebanon, but Israel went on to sponsor a Lebanese Christian militia called the South Lebanon Army (SLA), to control the country's southern region bordering Israel, and try to prevent Palestinian incursions.

OPERATION PEACE FOR GALILEE

In 1982, with the PLO still resident in Lebanon's shattered capital, Beirut, Israel invaded again. The catalyst was an assassination attempt on its ambassador in London - actually carried out, not by the PLO, but by the more extreme Abu Nidal faction. The Israeli attack, code-named Operation Peace for Galilee, was led by Ariel Sharon, then Defence Minister.

This time, the Israelis continued to advance until they surrounded Beirut, where they began a siege of the PLO positions. For two months, they pounded the capital. At that stage, Arafat and his men decided to spare the city's inhabitants more suffering, and pulled out.

HEZBOLLAH: THE ISLAM FACTOR

A group of Hezbollah fighters on parade.

Hezbollah was formed by Iranian Shi'ite militiamen sent to Lebanon after Israel's 1982 invasion. In the years since, it has proved to be one of the most ruthless pro-Palestinian groups, not least because of its members' claim to be acting in the name of religion. Moreover, its activities, which include providing basic social services, such as education, have endeared it to Palestinian refugees and the Lebanese Shi'ite community. Best known for its abduction of western hostages in the 1980s, Hezbollah first set out to wage a *jihad* (holy war) against Israel and to establish an Islamic Republic in Lebanon. More recently, it has won several seats in Lebanese elections, though its violence has continued.

RELIGIOUS VIOLENCE

Israel's military action helped to prolong the Lebanese disintegration. One consequence was the rise of a militant Shi'ite Muslim group, Hezbollah (the Party of God). In contrast to the secular PLO, Hezbollah has added a religious dimension to the Palestinian cause. Using the Shi'a cult of martyrdom, it has made the suicide bomber a weapon of choice against Israel and its allies, and has been joined in this by other radical Muslim groups such as Hamas and Islamic Jihad. But Muslims were also victims of the conflict in Lebanon. Indeed, Sharon was accused of allowing a war crime to take place when, after the murder of their leader Bashir Gemayel in 1983, Christian militiamen

The massacre at the Sabra camp, 1983.

entered the Palestinian refugee camps of Sabra and Shatila and massacred hundreds of refugees. Sharon denied that his men knew anything about the incident.

ISRAEL'S WITHDRAWAL

In 1985, the Israelis established a 'security zone' in southern Lebanon, and pulled most of their troops out of the country. Over the next fifteen years they launched further incursions. However, cross-border attacks and heavy losses led to the security zone also being evacuated in May 2000. Twenty-two years after it began, this messy and ultimately inconclusive episode had finally ended.

LEBANON

13 April 1975 Start of Lebanese civil war

14 March 1978 Operation Litani begins: Israeli invasion of southern Lebanon

19 March 1978 United Nations Resolution 425 passed; calls for Israel to withdraw

6 June 1982 Operation Peace for Galilee – Israel launches full-scale invasion of Lebanon

16-18 September 1982 Israel's Christian allies murder at least 800 Palestinians at refugee camps; Sharon later resigns as Defence Minister

23 October 1983 More than 200 US Marines killed in Shi'ite bomb attack in Beirut

15 January 1985 Israel announces withdrawal from most of Lebanon, but leaves SLA to patrol the southern border

25 July 1993 Israel launches Operation Accountability, aiming to end attacks by Hezbollah and the Popular Front for the Liberation of Palestine

24 May 2000 Israeli premier, Ehud Barak, completes full withdrawal from Lebanon

INTIFADA

Israeli military power may have kept a lid on both foreign aggression and the PLO, but it proved to be of limited use against a new kind of resistance in the 1980s: a mass uprising that pitched thousands of ordinary Palestinians against the Jewish state.

A Ticking Bomb

The *intifada* (awakening, or shaking off) was an extraordinary phenomenon, but it arose out of everyday tragedy and suspicion. Early in December 1987, a Jewish salesman was stabbed to death by an Arab, and just days later, an Israeli army vehicle ploughed into a group of Palestinians at the Jabalya refugee camp in Gaza, killing four of them. This may have been an accident, but Gaza inhabitants, themselves mostly refugees, saw it as deliberate revenge. They began a series of violent demonstrations, which soon spread to the West Bank.

The protests sparked off a much wider rebellion, fuelled by the pent-up anger of an entire generation that had by now grown up in the squalor of the refugee camps.

Stones Versus Bullets

The uprising continued for days, months - and eventually, years - mainly carried out by disillusioned young men and even children. It encompassed civil disobedience, strikes and riots; but its main tactic was stone-throwing. The Israeli military, alarmed by the breadth of support, responded by firing live rounds at the

A scene from the intifada: a stone-throwing Palestinian man confronts a group of Israeli soldiers.

REFUGEE CAMPS

The first Palestinian refugees, displaced by Israel's creation, lived under canvas. Today the camps are effectively permanent cities, but conditions remain poor. Around one-third of the three-and-a-half million refugees live in 59 sites run by the United Nations. Overcrowding, unemployment and poverty have helped to make them breeding grounds for hatred against Israel, especially among those raised in the camps, who have known no other life. The Palestinians demand the right to go back to their homes, now in Israeli territory. Israel refuses because this would threaten its Jewish majority.

Conditions in a United Nations Palestinian refugee camp.

crowds. The army insisted that these were aimed overhead or, as a last resort, at the legs; however, the Palestinian death toll quickly rose, and Israel - which was rebuked by the United Nations - saw its image suffer overseas.

A UNITED FRONT

The right-wing Likud government of Israel's latest prime minister - Yitzhak Shamir - attempted to crack down hard on the intifada: frequent border closures brought havoc to the Occupied Territories' economy; an 'iron fist' policy of mass arrests and evictions of Palestinians disrupted the lives of hundreds. But still the popular uprising went on, stretching the Israeli security services to the limits. Ordinary Palestinians had discovered a unity and motivation which had eluded all

previous allies of their cause. They were joined by the groups Islamic Jihad and Hamas, plus the PLO, which tried to claim the intifada for its own. Palestinian anger increased as a new wave of Jews arrived in Israel from the Soviet Union after 1988, contrasting with the refugees' own exclusion from their former homeland.

PAVING THE WAY TO PEACE

The intifada is commonly said to have lasted until 1993, by which time Shamir's government had been replaced by another administration, and peace negotiations were under way. Although other factors were at work in bringing about that attempted settlement, the intifada, which meant favourable publicity for the Palestinians while magnifying Israel's unease, seems to have played a part.

THE INTIFADA

8 December 1987 Start of first intifada, following vehicle accident in Gaza

19 December 1987 Worst violence in Jerusalem since 1967

8 January 1988 Signs of organised resistance emerge, as the 'Unified National Command of the Uprising' issues its first statements

28 March 1988 Israel seals off Occupied Territories

14 December 1988 Arafat renounces terrorism and recognises Israel's right to exist

28 September 1989 Islamic resistance group, Hamas, is outlawed

OSLO – HOPE AND DISAPPOINTMENT

In the early 1990s, a combination of waning PLO fortunes, the election of a strong but conciliatory prime minister in Israel, and vigorous American encouragement, provided an unprecedented opportunity for peace. But the Oslo Peace Accord that followed had powerful enemies.

UNPROMISING START

In 1988, the PLO feared its influence was declining. In response, it announced a radical new objective: to accept Israel's right to exist and pursue a negotiated settlement, trading Israeli-occupied land for peace. At first, Israel did not respond. The right-wing government considered Arafat's men to be terrorists, and would not negotiate with them. When the US convened a peace summit in Madrid in 1991, a non-PLO delegation had to be assembled on the Palestinian side.

DECLARATION OF PRINCIPLES

The breakthrough came in June 1992, with the election of a left-wing government in Israel, led by Yitzhak Rabin. By this time, the PLO was even more interested in peace: it had been much criticised by foreign backers over its support for the Iraqi invasion of Kuwait in 1990. So, while there was stalemate in Madrid, the two sides secretly opened another diplomatic channel, with the Norwegians as mediators. Here, they agreed a Declaration of Principles, stating their mutual recognition and desire to live in peace. Amid great fanfare, the declaration was signed at the White House on 13 September 1993. After so long, a Palestinian leader and an Israeli prime minister finally shook hands.

Watched by US President Bill Clinton, Yitzhak Rabin and Yasser Arafat shake hands on 13 September 1993.

> 'The battle for peace is the most difficult battle of our lives. It deserves our utmost efforts because the land of peace yearns for a just and comprehensive peace.'
>
> Yasser Arafat, 13 September 1993

OSLO'S LIMITATIONS

The deal hammered out in Norway, known as the Oslo Agreement, allowed Palestinian autonomy in some of the Occupied Territories, with Israel withdrawing its forces over a period of five years. The most difficult issues, including dismantling settlements and the status of Jerusalem, were to be shelved pending so-called 'final status' negotiations.

In 1994, a jubilant Yasser Arafat returned from exile and was subsequently elected president of a new Palestinian Authority. However, the peace process fell short of what some Palestinians wanted, especially as the autonomous areas remained crisscrossed by Jewish settlements and the roads linking them. Non-PLO militants such as the Islamic group, Hamas, sought to wreck the deal through a campaign of suicide bombings on Israel. Moreover, right-wing Israelis were furious at having to surrender occupied land. In November 1995, one of them – a young religious extremist called Yigal Amir – assassinated Prime Minister Yitzhak Rabin.

YITZHAK RABIN (1922-95), SOLDIER FOR PEACE

A former military Chief of Staff and hero of the Six-Day War, Yitzhak Rabin was no ordinary pacifist. His tough background enabled him to bargain with the PLO while maintaining the confidence of moderate Israelis. Rabin's actions arguably gave Israel its best chance of peace in half a century. His successor, Shimon Peres, was even more ready to be conciliatory, but he lacked Rabin's iron reputation, and the momentum towards a deal with the Arabs never recovered.

PEACE UNRAVELS

By 1996, the right-wing Likud Party was again in government. The new prime minister, Binyamin Netanyahu, felt that the peace deal threatened Israel's security. Although he did fulfil some of the agreed land exchanges, his premiership saw a return to colder relations with the Palestinians, amid continued violence and renewed Jewish settlement-building.

OSLO

30 October 1991 Start of historic peace talks in Madrid, between Israel and its Arab enemies

20 January 1993: Secret 'Oslo track' peace negotiations

13 September 1993 Israel and the PLO sign the Oslo Peace Accord

26 October 1994 Jordan makes peace with Israel

4 May 1994 Israel and the PLO sign the Gaza-Jericho Agreement in Cairo, preparing for Israeli withdrawal and establishment of the Palestinian Authority

1 July 1994 Arafat assumes power in Gaza

24 September 1995 The Taba Accord divides the West Bank into three zones, under Palestinian, Israeli and joint control

4 November 1995 Assassination of Rabin; succeeded by Peres

21 January 1996 Elections in the Palestinian territories; Arafat elected president

11 April 1996 Israel attacks Hezbollah bases in Lebanon

29 May 1996 Netanyahu wins Israeli elections

23 October 1998 Israel and the PLO sign the Wye River Deal whereby Israel was to withdraw from a further 13 per cent of the West Bank in return for Palestinian security guarantees; Israel later freezes this deal

As the 21st century dawned, the old hatred between Israelis and Palestinians was still very much in evidence. In more than fifty years of the state of Israel, the same basic conflict had endured and, indeed, worsened.

FADING HOPES

Binyamin Netanyahu's government fell in 1999 amid splits over the Oslo peace process, and another Labour premier, Ehud Barak, took office, pledging to end the Arab-Israeli conflict once and for all. By now though, the frustrations on both sides were very obvious. Barak made no progress on the most intractable 'final status' issues, such as who would rule Jerusalem, or on securing peace with Israel's northern neighbour, Syria, which demanded the return of the occupied Golan Heights in exchange for any deal. He spent two weeks with Yasser Arafat at Camp David trying to achieve a breakthrough, but none came, despite his offer to share sovereignty in parts of Jerusalem. Many observers blamed Arafat for the breakdown.

THE RISE OF ARIEL SHARON

Ehud Barak's political rivals in Israel exploited this lack of success. The Likud Party was now led by a veteran army officer, Ariel Sharon, who opposed the Oslo peace process. In September 2000, he toured the al-Aqsa/Temple Mount complex in Jerusalem, an area sacred to both Jews and Muslims. The Palestinians saw this as a demonstration of Jewish control over one of their holy sites. Their protests soon escalated into what became known as the second intifada. Sharon cited the unrest as proof that Israel's security had to come before a deal with Arafat.

ARIEL SHARON (1928-), ISRAEL'S WARRIOR

To supporters, Ariel Sharon is a tough champion of Israel. Critics call him a war criminal. Having seen action in all the Arab-Israeli wars, he helped form the right-wing Likud Party and first entered the Knesset in 1973. He was forced out of government after being rebuked over the Sabra and Shatila refugee camp massacres, which accompanied his 1982 invasion of Lebanon. Then, as Housing Minister in the 1990s, he oversaw huge settlement-building in the Occupied Territories. Having fought the PLO for decades, he rejected Yasser Arafat as a negotiating partner. But Mr Sharon has always been unrepentant, saying that what matters to Israel is security.

In February 2001, Ariel Sharon was elected prime minister. Under his administration, Israel turned its back on the idea of exchanging land for peace, in favour of rooting out Palestinian extremists. Sharon also oversaw the construction of a huge barrier to screen off much of the occupied West Bank. Made up of security fencing, barbed wire and even solid walls, this was conceived as a way of keeping Palestinian bombers out of Israel. However, Palestinians and international observers alike have complained that it further divides and isolates Arab territory. Critics believe it may also be intended as a *de facto* permanent border. Palestinian extremists have replied with even more suicide attacks.

A CENTURY OF CONFLICT

Following the suicide attacks on America on 11 September 2001, the Israelis compare their battle against Palestinian militants with the American-led 'war on terror'. But the Palestinians say that terrorism only thrives because of Israeli repression, and the desperation of a land-deprived people. Now the Americans themselves have called for a Palestinian state as the best way to ensure security.

Certainly, it is in everyone's interests to achieve a peaceful settlement: among the stated motives of the 11 September attackers was alleged American bias towards Israel and the perceived indifference of the West. The tragedy of

> **'The Palestinian state must be a reformed and peaceful and democratic state that abandons forever the use of terror. The government of Israel – as the terror threat is removed and security improves – must take concrete steps to support the emergence of a viable and credible Palestinian state.'**
>
> **US President George W Bush, March 2003**

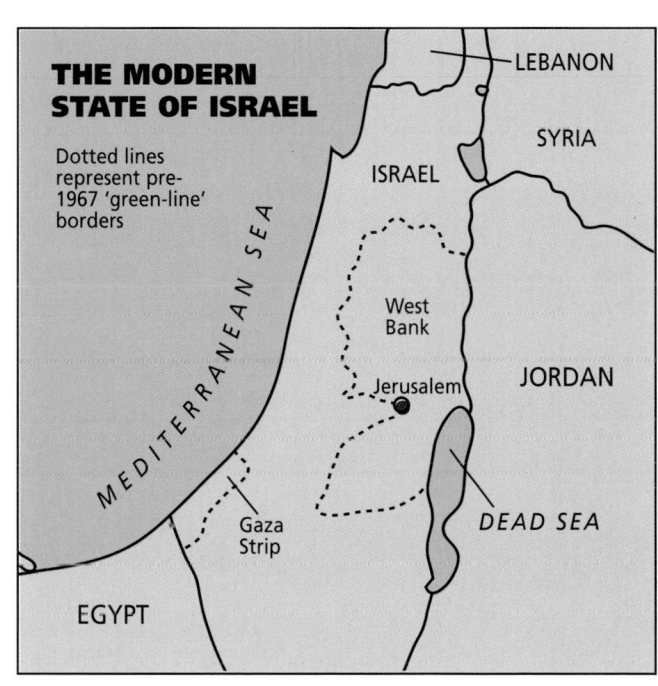

THE MODERN STATE OF ISRAEL

Dotted lines represent pre-1967 'green-line' borders

LEBANON
SYRIA
ISRAEL
MEDITERRANEAN SEA
West Bank
Jerusalem
JORDAN
Gaza Strip
DEAD SEA
EGYPT

the Middle East in the last century could spread much further in this one unless we try even harder to achieve a lasting peace.

INTO THE 21ST CENTURY	**28 September 2000** Sharon tours the al-Aqsa/ Temple Mount complex in Jerusalem; start of the second intifada	**6 February 2001** Ariel Sharon elected prime minister **11 September 2001** Al-Qaeda suicide attacks on New York and Washington kill 3,000	**March 2002** Pro-Palestinian attacks kill over 100 Israelis **28 March 2002** Israel reoccupies most of the West Bank	**April 2003** Publication of the 'Road Map' for peace, by America, the UN, the European Union and Russia

GLOSSARY

Aliya Zionist migration to Israel.

Annex To formally integrate a piece of occupied land into the occupying state.

Assimilation The process of merging with another culture. For a long time, educated Jews living in other countries, particularly those in western Europe, attempted to assimilate with their non-Jewish compatriots.

Camp David American Presidential retreat in Maryland, around 100 kilometres from the White House.

Communist bloc The grouping of communist states in central and eastern Europe centred upon the Soviet Union after World War II.

Crusades A series of religious wars between the 11th and 18th centuries, in which the Christians of Europe were called upon by the Papacy to attack the perceived enemies of their faith, but especially Muslims.

Diaspora Literally, 'dispersal': the global Jewish community created by Jews migrating from the lands of ancient Israel.

Final status The last phase of peace negotiations between Israel and the Palestinians, in which, under the Oslo Agreement, the most difficult issues were to be tackled.

Gaza Strip A narrow piece of land on the Mediterranean coast to the south-west of Israel, captured from Egypt in 1967.

Golan Heights Israeli-occupied Syrian territory overlooking the pre-1967 border with Israel, and therefore deemed to be of military significance.

Jerusalem Ancient city, holy to Christians, Jews and Muslims, and claimed by Israel as its capital.

Knesset The Israeli parliament.

League of Nations An international forum established after World War I with the aim of averting conflict. The League was undermined by the rise of fascism in the 1930s, and was succeeded by the United Nations after World War II.

Mandate Legal authority to govern a former colony, bestowed by the League of Nations.

Non-Aligned Movement A group of states that favoured having no alliance with either the United States or the Soviet Union during the Cold War.

Occupied Territories Lands captured by Israel, mainly during the Six-Day War. The term usually applies to East Jerusalem, the Gaza Strip, the Golan Heights and the West Bank of the River Jordan.

Ottomans Muslim dynasty based in Istanbul, which ruled an empire in the Middle East until its dissolution after World War I.

Palestinian Authority Autonomous Palestinian administration created under the Oslo Accord in 1994 to govern most of the Gaza Strip and parts of the West Bank.

Pan-Arabism A movement dedicated to forging a unified nation among the Arabs in response to colonialism and economic under-development. In the 1950s and 1960s, pan-Arabism's greatest proponent was the Egyptian president, Nasser.

Partition The formal division of a territory or country to produce two or more new political entities, and usually accompanied by a mass displacement of population between them.

Shi'a A branch of Islam which grew out of a dispute over the succession to the Prophet, Mohammed. Its followers believe a profound injustice was visited upon their preferred successor, Ali, and this has translated into a respect for martyrdom.

Shi'ites Followers of the Shi'a religion.

Sinai The desert peninsula beyond Israel's southern border belonging to Egypt.

Suez Canal A 19-kilometre long waterway in north-eastern Egypt that runs between the Mediterranean and Red Seas. Built in the 19th century, it is of major strategic importance since it allows shipping to bypass Africa.

United Nations The peace-seeking body formed in the wake of World War II as a successor to the League of Nations.

United Nations Resolution A decision of the United Nations. A resolution can be made by the UN General Assembly or the fifteen-member Security Council.

West Bank Territory to the west of the River Jordan, comprising most of the Palestinian land not under Israeli sovereignty after 1948. In 1967, Israel captured the West Bank from Jordan and occupied it.

Zionism A movement to recreate a physical Jewish state centred on Jerusalem.

INDEX